Conquer CyberOverload:

Get More Done, Boost Your Creativity, and Reduce Stress

Joanne Cantor, Ph. D.

CyberOutlook Press | Madison, Wisconsin

ISBN: 978-0-9842568-0-8

Library of Congress Control Number: 2009911768

First Edition

Book Design by Andrew Welyczko
Your Mind on Media Logo by Melissa Carlson

Disclaimer: Although every precaution has been taken in preparing this book, the author and publisher assume no responsibility for errors or omis-sions. No liability is assumed for damages that result, or are alleged to result, directly or indirectly from the use of the information contained herein. If you do not wish to be bound by the above, you may return this book with a re-ceipt to the publisher for a full refund.

For Bob and Alex

Contents

Preface
Why I Wrote This Book

All right. I admit it. I'm a recovering cyber-addict. Actually, my addiction to media started well before cyberspace. As early as my teenage years, I always wanted to have the TV or radio on, even when I was doing homework. By the time I started studying media effects in graduate school, people were concerned about what television and movies were doing to kids. They worried whether media violence made kids more aggressive or caused them to lose sleep; they wondered about the effects that advertising was having on children's values and eating habits; and they studied how educational television could foster healthy attitudes and help children learn. Over the course of my career, much of my research has dealt with these issues.

People are still discussing these themes, but by the time I had my own child, it wasn't just "old media" that concerned parents and researchers. Kids suddenly had access to computers, the Internet, cell phones, video games, and more. I found myself urging my teenage son not to spend too much time with fantasy sports, MySpace, and instant messaging, but as the offerings of the Internet exploded, I ended up competing with him for computer time. I became hooked on email and Internet surfing, and they took up more and more of my time. And as my son became an adult, and as the Internet, email, and smartphones came to increasingly dominate the lives of my friends and colleagues, I decided to broaden my research focus to look at the impact of the digital revolution on adults as well. My background of studying social, cognitive, and physiological psychology put me in a good position to understand the exciting advances that have been occurring in information processing and neuroscience.

I founded Your Mind on Media to provide keynotes and workshops to businesses and associations whose members are struggling to balance their desire to receive information, entertainment, and connectedness from cyberspace with their need to remain creative, productive, and psychologically healthy. My two most popular presentations, "You've Got (too much) Mail! – Preserving Productivity Under Information Overload," and "This is Your Mind on Media – Staying Sane in a Crazy Culture," have hit a resounding chord in my audiences. People often contact me months after hearing me speak, saying how the things they learned from me changed both their personal and professional lives in important and useful ways.

But there is so much to say on these topics, and research in these areas is growing so fast that a book is necessary to supplement the materials I can communicate orally. *Conquer CyberOverload* has grown out of my desire to know more (and to communicate more) about how the brain works and about how people can use that knowledge to make their lives saner and more productive in the Internet age.

My career straddles the academic and professional communities. As a professional speaker, I know that audiences want information in easily digestible form that is delivered in ways that involve the audience and provide new insights. As a researcher, I know that anyone can make any claim, but that to be credible, claims need to be backed up by solid research evidence. To satisfy both concerns, I've written the book in an easily readable form, giving only enough information about research for the reader to understand the conclusions. But I have also included notes at the back to enable people to look up the studies I'm citing.

I wanted this book to be short and full of easily followed recommendations so that busy people would have the time to benefit from it. In my own life, I have adopted many of these strategies. Although I keep up with what I think is important, I am no longer constantly connected. I enjoy quiet times and find they are psychologically rejuvenating and intellectually nourishing. Cutting back on multitasking and task-switching has certainly improved my memory and allowed me to get much more done. And I feel that my creativity has flourished. I hope this book does the same for you.

Introduction

Are You Suffering from CyberOverload?

- Do you find yourself getting less done, now that you have constant access to limitless information?
- When you're in the middle of a conversation or a meeting, is it difficult for you to *not* take that cell-phone call or check your Blackberry?
- When you're trying to get something done, is it hard for you to stop going online to see the latest in what's happening in the world?
- Do entertainment and news programs leave you feeling agitated and stressed out rather than informed and entertained?
- Are you so busy and so attached to technology that you don't even have time to think?

In short, are your communication habits making you feel more connected and in control—or are they controlling YOU and stressing you out?

CyberOverload happens when our gadgets and constant electronic linkages interfere with our ability to lead the life we want. We may be so addicted to the Internet that we can't accomplish what we want to do. We may be so overloaded with information that we can't come up with new ideas when we're trying to be creative. And we may be so stressed out from what we see in the media that our emotional and physical health suffer.

Do you own your gadgets or do they own you?

This book is about how we can overcome CyberOverload to enhance our productivity, our creativity, and our sanity, while still benefiting from the great gifts that technology has to offer.

■ *Conquer CyberOverload* is Intended for Several Audiences

- People who want to get more done at work, at home, or on the go
- Managers who want to motivate their employees toward greater productivity
- Creative types who want to increase their capacity for innovation
- Anyone who wants to balance their technological connectedness with their personal or professional goals

1

How the Digital Revolution Changed Everything

> "The digital revolution is far more significant than the invention of writing or even of printing."
>
> Computing pioneer Douglas Engelbart
> (inventor of the mouse)

You may be old enough to remember this

... or it all may sound like ancient history.

Once upon a time:

- If the phone rang and no one was there to answer it, you never knew about it unless they called back.
- The only mail that arrived came in envelopes once a day.
- Phones were only as mobile as the length of the cord that plugged them into the wall.
- If you wanted to know the answer to something,

you had to have an encyclopedia or go to the
library to check out *books*.
- You had to walk all the way across the living room
to change the TV channel.

Clearly, we're living in an entirely different world from
the one I grew up in a half-century ago.

....

*When I was a freshman in college, I wrote my papers with a
pen on a yellow pad, and I used a manual typewriter to create
a final copy. I had to learn to use a slide-rule to perform calculations in Chemistry. By the time I learned statistics in graduate school, twenty classmates and I had to share two slow mechanical calculators (with rows of numbered buttons like an
old-fashioned cash register). I did have access to a computer,
but I had to walk four blocks to feed my punch-cards into an
IBM machine the size of a large building, and then come back
the next day to pick up the printout of my results. I had to type
my Ph.D. dissertation on a typewriter (by then, thankfully, it
was an electric one). And I don't even want to think about
how difficult it was to correct an error in typing.*

....

■ The Digital Dream

Today, just about everything I need is on my laptop. I can do
data analyses in an instant that are more sophisticated than
the ones an old IBM mainframe used to take a day to do.
Word-processing has made creating and editing manu-

scripts incredibly easier. And I have access to information from all over the world. What's more, that information is digitized, so I can learn what I want to know by just putting a word or phrase into a search engine. And these new devices provided by the digital revolution have also created a communication revolution. With our cell phones, laptops, and ipods, we've got everything at our fingertips. And we're never alone because we can call, text, email, IM, social-network, and tweet each other endlessly.

The constant connectivity that our gadgets provide can be wonderful. Our cell phones can rescue us if our car breaks down on a lonely road at night [spoiling a classic premise for horror stories]; they can help us meet up with friends or colleagues at a huge event when our schedules change; and they can help us contact our teenage children when they're not where we thought they'd be. With social networking, we can make new business contacts and stay connected or re-connect with friends and family from long ago. We can use the Internet to find everything we can think of, and with our smartphones and PDAs, we can command access to an infinite amount of information without even getting out of bed!

■ On the Other Hand...

But there's a downside to this constant connectivity, and it certainly has become apparent in business. More and more, people are worrying that these marvelous technological advances have interfered with our creativity and productivity to an alarming extent. The term "cyberloafing" has been coined to describe the problem of employees' engaging in recreational Internet surfing or personal messaging when they're supposed to be working. But even *motivated* employees find their productivity decreasing as a function of distractions that have become unrelenting because of technology.

It's not just Cyber-Loafing that's going on. Even dedicated employees are distracted by the ready availability of limitless information.

The management consulting firm BASEX estimates that unnecessary interruptions cost U. S. businesses $650 billion per year. This loss is considered such a crisis that companies like Microsoft, Intel and IBM formed the Information Overload Research Group (www.iorgforum.org) in 2008. IORG's tag line is: "Reducing Information Pollution." These businesses are aware of the irony that the very innovations they have introduced to increase productivity are becoming a huge obstacle to efficiency. And they are looking for solutions.

In the personal sphere, the problems of round-the-clock connectedness are seen every day. Many people lament the toll their technological devices take on their serenity and their personal relationships.

. . . .

Several years ago my friend's daughter, who worked for an investment bank, proudly showed me her wonderful new Blackberry, which was a perk of her job. One year later, that wonderful gadget had become her @%#*! Blackberry, because of the way it allowed her job to follow her everywhere and never let her relax.

. . . .

People are looking for a variety of solutions. In 2008, a writer for the *New York Times* confessed to his "techno-addiction" and said he had instituted a "secular Sabbath"—one day a week in which he turns off all his electronic devices in order to reconnect with himself. Some people are talking about undergoing cyber-detox, trying to break their connection to technology for at least a short time. But breaking the techno-habit is not easy.

■ Why Cyber-Connectedness is So Addictive

. . . .

A recent video documentary titled Disconnected *asked three college students to give up their computers (and all computer use) for a month, and then followed them around to witness the effects. Although the students' vows of disconnection caused disruptions in their classwork, what they said they missed the most was email, which was their Number 1 way of communicating with their friends. They also felt left out of what was happening because they knew that everybody else was online. Finally, they said they felt bored, because it had been their habit to use* any free moment *to check out what was going on in cyberspace.*

. . . .

Our cyber-connection tools have such a powerful hold on us because they meet some very basic needs that were met in other ways before these tools were invented.

One need is a sense of belonging—we love to hear from our friends and family and other people we admire. A generation ago, people who were away at school or at camp would look forward to the time of day when the mail was sorted, and the people who received mail always felt better than those who did not. It made them feel important or loved, or at least recognized. Now, of course, we can have our antennae out for the electronic mail carriers every minute of the day.

Our gadgets are also enticing because curiosity is a major motivator. It is easy to pique our curiosity, and besides, we don't want to be the last to know about

Our gadgets meet some very basic needs. some important (or even trivial) event of interest. And with the vast expanse of the Internet, there is always something new, and there is always something of interest.

Finally, people don't like to be bored, and when there is such a ready antidote to boredom at your fingertips, getting rid of boredom is not a problem.

■ Understanding Our Brains

So what's wrong with us? Why can't we just adapt to these wonderful new tools—taking what they add to our social relationships, our knowledge, and our amusement without suffering unwanted side effects? Why do these tools sometimes reduce, rather than enhance our productivity and creativity, and why do they stress us out?

The answer can be found by understanding the way our brains work—what they can and cannot do and why some of the feats that technology is asking us to perform are so difficult. The contemporary human brain is very similar to the brain of homo sapiens who lived 40,000 years ago, who had to contend with a very different environment. Although it's true that the connections in our brains are altered every time we learn something new, **The design of our** there are basic characteristics of the brain **brains is suited for** that have not changed in thousands of years. **a more low-tech** It turns out that it's easier to modify our **environment.** habits than to alter basic principles of how the mind works. The more we know about how the brain functions, then, the better we can learn to adapt our environment, including technology, to serve our needs the best.

2

"Now Where Was I...?"
Why Multitasking Is Counterproductive

"Multitasking is the art of distracting yourself from two things you'd rather not be doing by doing them simultaneously."

(Variously Attributed)

One effect of our powerful, portable electronic gadgets is that we're multitasking much of the time. We're checking our emails while talking on our cell phones; we're balancing our checkbooks while watching TV; we're web-surfing for news while we're writing a memo. The possible combinations of tasks are endless. And we often don't limit ourselves to two tasks.

■ Understanding Multitasking

In some ways our brains are always multitasking. Right now, your brain is making your heart pump blood, helping you breathe and digest your food, and performing many other functions that keep you alive and alert. These background tasks normally do not interfere with your ability to read this book or write an article or enjoy your favorite TV show. The reason there's no conflict is that these brain activities do not require your conscious attention. There is no explicit information-processing or decision-making going on in your brain's control of your digestion, for example. In fact, we can walk and chew gum at the same time because both of these activities are performed relatively automatically. We don't usually have trouble walking and talking at the same time either: We can have an involved conversation with a friend or co-worker while taking a walk. However, if we get lost and suddenly have to figure out where we are or have to make a decision about where to turn, our conversation will take a back seat until we have safely returned to the right path and our walking is back on "auto-pilot."

. . . .

My first experience with the perils of multitasking came in high school, when I attempted to do two things at once that I thought should not conflict. I wanted to practice a poem that I had memorized for school, and I had to set my mother's hair. Since I had the poem down pat and I had set my mother's hair many times before, I thought I'd save time by practicing the poem out-loud while I put the rollers in my mother's hair. This turned out to be totally impossible: The moment I'd reach for a roller, I'd completely lose those well-memorized words; and if I concentrated on the words, I couldn't make any progress on her hair. I finally had to give up and do the two tasks separately. I remember this episode so well because it was so surprising. Since reciting a poem involves words only, and hair-setting involves no words, why should they conflict?

· ·

Experts in information-processing and brain researchers now know that our brains cannot focus attention on two things at once. Molecular biologist John Medina, who has written a wonderful book called *Brain Rules,* says "it is literally impossible for our brains to multitask when it comes to paying attention." What is really happening when we seem to be multitasking is that we are rapidly switching our attention back and forth between tasks. When I use the term multitasking in this book, it will refer to attempts to do two or more things at once, but with this understanding that attention is being switched between the tasks.

Our attention can't multitask. It can only switch back and forth between tasks.

What's Involved in Task-Switching?

Our brains switch tasks a lot. In fact, our brains are designed in such a way that our attention is easily grabbed by something that quickly changes in our environment, and this has obvious survival value. When our species' ancestors were living on the Savannas of Africa, if the image of a sabretooth tiger racing toward them hadn't caught their attention, we wouldn't be here today. With this *involuntary attention* we heed any sudden loud noise or flashy display. Advertisers know this, and that's why television and other media are so full of rapidly changing images and sounds.

Our brains can also focus on relatively stable content for extended periods of time, but this *directed attention* takes much more controlled processing. Controlled attention is especially difficult in a noisy environment that's full of distractions. The part of our brain that controls our attention is referred to as the "executive network," and it is in the prefrontal cortex, a highly advanced part of our brain. The executive network determines not only what we pay attention to, but also what responses we inhibit in order to pay attention effectively. Under conditions of distraction, there's a lot of work for the executive network to do.

In my productivity workshops, rather than focusing on how often people multitask or on how much money businesses lose because of multitasking, I allow the members of the audience to experience the challenges of multitasking themselves by walking them through a series of brain exercises.

The Stroop Test. The first demonstration I do is a classic psychology exercise called the Stroop Test, which illustrates some of the difficulties encountered when the brain needs to switch back and forth between two modes of processing. In this test, I show people a series of words flashed on a computer screen. All the words refer to colors (red, blue, green, etc.), and the letters of the words are displayed in a color that is different from the color-meaning of the word. For example, the word "red" is shown in blue letters. (See the back cover of this book for an example.) The person taking the test is told to ignore what the word says and call out the *color of the letters* as quickly as possible. This turns out to be difficult, because once we know how to read, we automatically read the words. So, in this task, we have to inhibit that first inclination to focus on the word that the letters spell, and instead call out the word that refers to the color of the letters. Each time a new word comes on the screen, our brains go back to their habitual mode of reading the word, which again must be inhibited as we switch our attention to the letters' color and then call up the word that identifies that color. Now, imagine that instead of words, what was flashed on the screen was just a colored dot. In that case, you could much more easily yell out the color because you would not need to switch from word-reading mode to color-identifying mode.

If you try the Stroop test, you will find that it puts an extra cognitive load on your brain; it's not easy, and it can be stressful, especially if you're trying to do it fast and without making mistakes.

A Task-Switching Exercise. Another way I make my audiences experience task switching is to perform an exercise I adapted from Dave Crenshaw's book, *The Myth of Multitasking.* Here are two well-known sequences of words, one from our National Anthem and the other from a nursery rhyme:

Oh, say can you see by the dawn's early light. What so proudly we hailed at the twilight's last gleaming.

Hickory Dickory Dock. The mouse ran up the clock. The clock struck one, the mouse ran down. Hickory Dickory Dock.

Figure 1. Task-Switching Exercise,
Adapted from Dave Crenshaw, *The Myth of Multitasking*

SINGLE-TASK	Oh, say can you see, by the dawn's early light, what so proudly we hailed at the twilight's last gleaming.
	1.
	Hickory Dickory Dock. The mouse ran up the clock. The clock struck one, the mouse ran down. Hickory Dickory Dock.
	2.
MULTI-TASK	Oh, say can you see, by the dawn's early light, what so proudly we hailed at the twilight's last gleaming.
	3.
	Hickory Dickory Dock. The mouse ran up the clock. The clock struck one, the mouse ran down. Hickory Dickory Dock.
	4.

I give my audiences a form that looks like Figure 1. First, I time them single-tasking the exercise. They write the words from the National Anthem in Space 1, and then the words from the nursery rhyme in Space 2. Following that, I have them task-switch, by writing the first word of the national anthem in Space 3, followed by the first word of the nursery rhyme in Space 4; then back up to Space 3 for the second word of the national anthem, back to Space 4 for the second word of the nursery rhyme and so on, alternating the two tasks, word by word. You won't be surprised to learn that it takes much longer to multitask this exercise than to single-task it. You can try this yourself at home. After that, for a really intense, brain-stressing experience, try task-switching these two expressions from memory, reciting them out-loud without writing the words down. Of course, this exercise ex-aggerates the rate of typical task-switching. But people switch back and forth more often than you might expect. One estimate says that people at work change their task fo-cus *every three minutes!*

What you will discover if you try this task-switching ex-ercise is that one of the major stumbling blocks is remem-bering where you were every time you re-turn to the task you just left. And it's very inefficient and often error-prone. Now imagine two tasks that are more complex competing with one another, like writing a business memo and emailing a friend. The greater the level of complexity and the more original the content you have to cre-ate, the worse the interference.

Our brains cannot multitask, and when we rapidly switch back and forth between tasks, both tasks suffer.

Research shows very conclusively that multitasking—that is, performing two tasks that require attention at the same time—is ineffective. Our brains cannot multitask; they can only switch back and forth between the tasks, and both tasks suffer. In fact, whenever we are interrupted or even when we switch back and forth between two tasks volun-tarily, we lose both time and accuracy. This is undoubtedly why executive coach Russell Bishop calls multitasking "half-tasking." In other words, when you're dual-tasking *you're giving it your half!*

Where's the Bottleneck? — The Strain on Working Memory

One reason why multitasking (or task-switching) is so difficult is that it calls upon a brain resource that's extremely limited. Working memory (sometimes also called short-term memory) is memory that holds brief tidbits of information in consciousness for short periods of time. The most common example used to demonstrate working memory is looking up a number in the phone book. We are able to hold about seven numbers in mind briefly, but we must do something immediately—like repeating them or writing them down—to keep them from disappearing from our thoughts. With task-switching we call upon working memory to remind us where we were when we left the previous task; otherwise, we have to review what we did earlier in order to refresh our memory. You might think of the role of working memory in task-switching as akin to thought juggling. We have to keep a certain number of "thought balls" in the air at the same time to make any progress. This is difficult when we're reading and especially difficult when we're writing or creating something new. Even over the course of reading or writing a sentence or paragraph, you have to hold the beginning in memory in order to fully comprehend the end. You may notice this clearly when you're reading a newspaper that splits an article between pages mid-sentence, forcing you to scan through a number of headlines before finding the continuation.

When you switch back and forth between tasks, it takes time for your brain to remember what was going on with the earlier task. If you're often saying to yourself "now, where was I?" it means you're task-switching too much. In addition, the task-switching delay may be even longer because every time you switch tasks, you're more likely to be further distracted by something else and postpone returning to the first task even further.

Who Multitasks the Best?

There are a number of current debates about multitasking. It is a commonly held notion that women can multitask more easily than men. I think this idea arose because women, particularly women with children, have traditionally been responsible for performing many tasks at once. However, research has not been able to demonstrate any consistent evidence of women's superiority over men in multitasking.

Young adults are better at multitasking because they have a larger working memory capacity.

There is some truth to the notion that young adults can multitask more effectively than older adults. The underlying factor is that they have a larger working memory capacity so they don't lose as much information every time they switch. Researchers estimate that working memory reaches its peak at about the age of twenty-five and then begins a slow decline. So, as we age, the cost of switching back and forth between tasks becomes higher.

Some people have also argued that members of the current younger generation are better multitaskers because they have grown up in a cyberspace environment and their brains have been transformed by their digital experiences. However, working memory cannot expand a great deal as a function of training. And although some people contend that we can improve our multitasking abilities with intense practice, new research suggests that this may not be true. A 2009 study out of Stanford tried to demonstrate that frequent multitaskers would perform better than infrequent multitaskers in situations involving two simultaneous tasks.

They compared the performance of students who said they multitasked a lot to a group who said they hardly ever multitasked on three tests that involved dual-tasking or task-switching, and *the frequent multitaskers performed more poorly on all three tests.* The researchers were shocked because they expected to find at least one task that the high multitaskers would excel at, but they were unable to. Apparently, then, people do not multitask because they are good at it; perhaps they do it because they find single-tasking boring and multitasking more stimulating.

Frequent multitaskers are poor multitaskers!

A further blow to multitasking comes from a study out of UCLA, which demonstrated that multitasking and single-tasking involve different brain processes and that learning while multitasking produces a lower level of understanding. Participants engaged in some learning trials while single-tasking and other learning trials while dual-tasking. When tested later *using the same procedures they had learned with*, there wasn't a big difference in performance for things learned while single-tasking vs. multitasking. However, when participants were tested for the same learning *in a different context*, performance was much better for single- than dual-tasked trials. In other words, when the learning had taken place in the context of a second task, people could perform the learned behavior, but they were much less able to identify the rules underlying what they were doing. Brain imaging revealed that different areas of the brain had been active under single-tasked as opposed to multitasked learning. Learning while multitasking involved *implicit processes* similar to forming a habit without consciousness of what is being learned. Learning while single-tasking involved utilizing working memory, and what was learned was more flexible and involved more abstract, generalizable knowledge.

In summary, although the degree of interference that multitasking exerts on a particular outcome may vary as a function of characteristics of the two tasks, multitasking generally slows down progress and interferes with the accuracy and quality of the work being attempted. Therefore, even if it's possible to

Multitasking is akin to using your left hand if you're right handed.

improve your multitasking skills with practice, you should still do much better when you're single-tasking. This may be considered analogous to the fact that if you're right-handed, you can work hard to train your left hand to do the things that your right hand does easily. However, you are unlikely to get to the point where your left-hand is equal to your right. So, no matter what your age, you'll do a better and more efficient job if you concentrate on one thing at a time when you need to get things done.

Interruptions Create the Same Problems

Because most of the technology we use is designed to notify us immediately when someone is trying to contact us, we are being interrupted more and more frequently throughout the day. This usually means that we interrupt whatever we're doing to at least check to see who's trying to contact us, and for many people, it means answering that call or checking the content of the message even if we're busy doing something important. Whether we just check to see who it's from or we explore what's in the message, we're task-switching, and this creates the same burden on our productivity that multitasking does. Repeated interruptions also have implications for our stress levels, something we'll come back to in Chapter 4.

■ How to Get Things Done in Our Hyper-Connected Environment

What we've learned so far in this chapter is that our attention is easily attracted by new information that arrives suddenly, and that if we want to get anything done, we need to focus on one thing at a time. The more often we are interrupted, either by other people or by irrelevant content, the less we get done and the lower the quality of the work that we do complete. So, the first bit of advice is to give yourself generous swaths of time during the day in which interruptions are kept to a minimum. Of course, you can't (and probably don't want to) focus on one thing all day, but you *can* be the one who decides when the interruptions should come.

Your best strategy is to focus on one thing at a time.

Limit Your Interruptions from Other People

Can you find some time during the day when you're totally incommunicado and you can ignore calls, emails, texts, and the like? Perhaps you haven't been able to do this, and many people have legitimate concerns that a particular type of urgent message must get through in all circumstances. We'll come back to this point below, with some recommendations on how to accommodate these concerns and still have some reasonably quiet work periods.

First, determine what length of uninterruptible time works for you as a starting point, and then commit to turning off your email, text, social-networking, cell phone, and so on, for that period. You may even want to close the door to your office or find a work area where most people will not be looking for you. Rather than posting a "Do Not Disturb" sign, you might want to leave a sign that tells people when you'll be back.

Get to work on your project, and when that itch to check email or explore online happenings strikes, resist it with the knowledge of how much more you're getting done this way. When your predetermined work period is over, go ahead and check your emails and other messages if you need to, deleting messages that are spam or simply unnecessary, returning those that should be answered right away, and deciding when the others should be dealt with. The essence of this technique is that *you are the decider* of when these communications take place.

Instead of using a time-limit for your uninterruptible time, you may prefer to set a goal to be accomplished, such as finishing a particular portion of a project. The idea is that your interruptions come at a reasonable time to take a break—you can't work endlessly on one thing without needing a breather anyway.

Handling Your Incommunicado Worries. You may be understandably worried about turning off your technological devices for any period of time for fear that an important potential communication just can't wait—a call from your child's school or an aging relative, perhaps, or from a work supervisor or a client who absolutely needs you at that moment. But there are ways to accommodate these "drop-everything" contacts without dropping everything for everybody.

The first thing you should do is to compile your own (hopefully limited) list of your drop-everything contacts. Then design a system for these people to contact you that differs from what you use for everyone else. For personal emergencies, you might want to give those people the phone number of an assistant or colleague who is willing to interrupt you if it's really urgent. For work contacts, the situation may be a bit more complicated. In many offices, people have their email on all the time, and the email program is set to check and display new messages every minute. Many people expect an immediate response to emails, and therefore, employees may feel they simply cannot *not* check every email as it comes in, just in case it's their supervisor or an important client.

Solving this situation may need to involve discussions about company communication policies. Rather than expecting everyone to monitor their email constantly, a manager could decide that a phone call is more appropriate than an email when an immediate response is needed. Or, supervisors who want their employees to be productive while still being able to reach them by email, might set up a separate, private email account that can get through even when other emails are temporarily blocked.

What If It's Oprah or Bill Gates or a Potential New Client?

Maybe you've just *got* to know who's trying to contact you, even if it means just looking at the sender of an email or the caller ID of a phone message. Well, that's better than picking up every phone call or opening every message as it arrives. And what about that new client or potential donor who calls out of the blue and whose name or number you can't recognize? Well, there are advantages to letting calls like that go to voicemail anyway. Even if you check that message right away, you can first make a note on what you're working on to remind you

Letting your phone go to voicemail can benefit you in more ways than one.

where you were when you left it. More importantly, when you return that call, you can be sure to have all the information you need at your fingertips—rather than hemming and hawing while you search for the answers to that important person's questions.

....

In June of 2008, an employee of Intel reported the results of a pilot study in which 300 engineers and managers agreed to minimize interruptions and distractions every Tuesday morning by setting their email and IM clients offline, sending their phone calls to voicemail, avoiding meetings, and putting "do not disturb" signs on their doors. The purpose was to allow four straight hours of "thinking time" once a week. The pilot reported "markedly positive results" and was deemed "successful in improving effectiveness, efficiency and quality of life" for employees in a variety of job roles. There was enthusiasm for extending the practice to more employees in other groups.

. . . .

Limit Your Self-Generated Interruptions

Other people present only a part of the interruption problem. The other part is you yourself, when random thoughts pop into your head—"oh, I meant to find a present for Lori's baby" or "I promised Bob I'd locate a hotel for our upcoming trip." These thoughts often come while you're trying to work on something else. You may worry you'll forget to follow through on that thought, and it's so convenient and so tempting to go online right then to get it done. But instead, keep your focus on what you're doing and simply have an old-fashioned pad and pen by your computer to jot down these ideas, which can be acted upon during one of your breaks, if appropriate, or later, at home.

Another thought that sometimes pops into your head while you're working is "I wonder what's happening right now that I don't know about"—sports outcomes, political events, stock prices, or what your friends are doing. Because you can usually learn the answer with a click of your mouse, it can be tough to delay gratification of that urge to know it now. It's especially difficult not to succumb to these temptations if you are using the Internet to explore something related to what you're working on. One suggestion to reduce the temptation is to be careful in choosing your default browser home page. I used to have mine set to a frequently updated news site, so whenever I went online for a legitimate research purpose, I couldn't help being distracted by the latest world happenings and then wandering off to another site instead of pursuing what I went online for in the first place. Choose a site for your home page that doesn't change often, so you'll be less likely to be distracted.

It's tough to overcome that urge to know everything NOW.

When you do go on the web for research that you're working on, try to keep your focus on what you went there for. If something less relevant but interesting should emerge, bookmark the site and return to it later. If you're at work, be sure to find out what works best for you, within the rules and customs of the organization you work for.

Forget Multitasking

When it comes to multitasking, just don't do it! It only slows you down and gets in your way. Whenever you find yourself in a multitasking situation, notice what's going on in your brain—how often you're switching, how much you're losing, how often you're re-starting something you've already begun—and you may automatically move toward focusing on one thing at a time. For starters, try single-tasking something that you usually multitask, even for a brief period of time. You'll be amazed at how much more effective (and less stressed) you'll be, and you're likely to try it again, for longer.

Some of these suggestions may seem difficult if your cyber habits are anything like mine used to be. But the good news is that even if you only follow this advice for very short periods of time, you will benefit. Once you try focusing for as little as 15 to 30 minutes at a time, you may find you like the results so much that you increase your quiet times more and more. Tables 1 and 2 summarize these suggestions for mastering your interruptions and getting more done.

PRACTICAL STEPS ❶

Be the Master of Your Interruptions

Of course, you can't focus solidly on one thing all day, but YOU CAN be the one to decide when the interruptions come.

When you need to get things done, create a time-specified private zone and limit interruptions from other people:

- Decide which people are your drop-everything contacts and find a way for them to get through to you in all circumstances.
- Turn your email off, and schedule email-checking breaks every two hours (or whatever interval works for you) or at a natural break in your work.
- Check phone messages on a limited schedule (if necessary, put your message-checking schedule in your outgoing message)—or make judicious use of caller-ID for emergencies.
- Let people know when you'll be available and they're more likely to tolerate your withdrawal.
- Coordinate with the people who work with you to make sure your new communication habits work for them.

PRACTICAL STEPS ❷

Limit Your Self-Generated Interruptions When You're Trying to Get Things Done

- Keep a note-pad by your computer to jot down random thoughts that pop-up, unrelated to your task.

- Limit web-browsing to what's essential to make progress at that moment; if you come upon something interesting but unrelated, bookmark it for later.

- Set your default browser page to something boring (not a site that has constantly changing, fascinating content, like a news, gossip, or sports site).

- Resist the urge to message-check or browse by reminding yourself of how much more you're accomplishing. It will all be there for you when you have the time.

- Follow your company's policies on web use or negotiate a policy with your supervisor that works for both you and your company.

3

"I'm Drowning in it!"
How Information Overload Blocks Creativity

"Creativity is a lot like looking at the world through a kaleidoscope. You look at a set of elements, the same ones everyone else sees, but then reassemble those floating bits and pieces into an enticing new possibility."

Business Guru Rosabeth Moss Kanter

Thus far, we have been talking about two related effects of constant connectivity that interfere with productivity—multitasking and interruptions. A third common effect is information overload. Because our technological devices make endless bits of information available to us at the touch of a button, and each new bit of information provides avenues to arrays of even more information, it's easy to become overloaded and overwhelmed.

Here's a simple way to experience how even a minor form of information overload can get in the way of accomplishing something:

Take a task as mundane as mental arithmetic. Start
with the number 93 and, without writing anything
down, subtract 7; then keep subtracting 7 until the
number you end up with is in the 30's. Try it for a
minute. If you do, you'll find yourself focusing
inward: You may close your eyes or at least you'll
look up at the ceiling or in the direction of something static and unchanging, so that the visual
images your brain receives do not interfere with
the work it's performing. Processing even simple
moving images while doing mental calculations
would interfere with your computational ability.
Now try doing the same exercise with the TV on.

Information overload from having too many simultaneous inputs can interfere with everyday tasks like reading an
article or balancing your checkbook. Another form of information overload—having too much information to consider at once—is especially counterproductive when you're
trying to be creative.

■ Having That Insight

When I talk about creativity, I'm talking about trying to
come up with something new. You're not simply following
the instructions for completing a task, you're trying to "think
outside the box." You're attempting to produce a new idea or
trying to put things together in a novel way, or trying to find
a new method of solving an old problem. You may be writing a report that synthesizes data in an original manner, for

example, or coming up with an innovative ad campaign, developing a new software solution, or writing a book.

If this is the kind of work you do, you undoubtedly have had the experience of pulling together a multitude of facts and ideas from a variety of sources and then trying to get a handle on where they all lead. Sometimes, you end up with so much information that you don't know where to go next. You're looking for the structure that fits everything together, or you're looking for some inventive relationship between the various pieces of information you've gathered. What you're experiencing is the inability to see the forest for the trees, because your mind is so overloaded with information.

Sometimes, you work and work on this pile of information, and you can't make any progress, so, in frustration, you give up, at least for a while, and decide to return to it later, or maybe the next day. Often what happens is that the next day, new relationships or new steps suddenly present themselves, seemingly out of the blue. Today, the forest that had been obscured by too many trees is staring you smack in the face, and you can't understand how you missed it yesterday. What you've experienced here, is what

When you can't see the forest for the trees, you're experiencing information overload.

some writers refer to as "insight"—that sudden "aha!" experience that permits you to make a creative move.

Why does information overload interfere? First, there's the working memory problem I referred to in Chapter 2. Since we can hold only a small number of ideas in consciousness at one time, it may be impossible to perceive the "big picture" when too much information is jumbled together. If we keep seeking more and more information—which is so easy to do now that it's only a click away—we only make matters worse. So learning when to stop seeking new information is important.

....

Our brains don't like too much information: Research shows that although people like to have choices when making a decision, if they are given too many choices, they feel less happy about their ultimate decision and are less satisfied with the decision-making process itself. One consumer study showed this dramatically. When supermarket customers were offered samples of three different types of jam, one-third of them purchased a jar of the jam. But when they were offered 25 different choices, only 3% ended up purchasing a jar.

....

Although there are a variety of definitions of creativity, many people think of creativity as the process of forming new links between previously separate ideas or pieces of information. The question is, then, what can we do to help our brain make those innovative connections that will move us forward?

Our brains are a storehouse of thousands and thousands of bits of information that might be related to the solution to our problem. The more information we have, ironically, the harder it may be to find that important piece that can help us make the next move. Think about finding that suit you haven't worn in a long time by looking in your over-stuffed closet vs. finding it in your suitcase. No contest.

Of course, the solution is *not* to keep your mind relatively fact-free so there's little to sort through. One approach is to organize your knowledge very well so that you can easily find what you're looking for. But what if you're looking for a creative solution and don't know exactly what you're seeking? What if you're searching for that unexpected, previously unconnected idea that might provide an innovative spark? One problem with tightly focusing on a problem is that you're unlikely to encounter that serendipitous thought that creates a new idea.

....

Years, ago, I was working on a grant proposal to study how children's fears are affected by the mass media. I had been urged to take a developmental focus, so I spent weeks reading the theories of the most influential child development experts. I remember spending one entire Saturday in my campus office, reading and taking notes, trying to find a connection, but nothing emerged. I had promised myself to take a break at the end of the day, however, by going to a political fundraiser. I left feeling frustrated that I hadn't accomplished anything, but on the way from my office to the parking lot, the idea of how to relate Piaget's developmental stages to what frightens children at different ages hit me like a ton of bricks. It was suddenly so obvious that I couldn't believe someone hadn't already proposed or studied it. My resulting proposal led to years of grant funding, many articles and awards, and a book for parents. I believe that that moment of breaking away was as important as the hours with my head in books.

....

A 2008 *New Yorker* article by Jonah Lehrer, author of *How We Decide*, reports what neurophysiologists are learning about that "eureka" moment, when we suddenly make a breakthrough. Researchers looking inside the brain during problem solving have noted that the areas of the brain that become active first are those dealing with focus and executive function, like the prefrontal cortex. But after a period of tight focus on the problem and just before the aha! moment occurs, researchers have observed a state of brain relaxation, which loosens the tight focus and makes the brain more likely to make new and *distant* connections between previously unrelated areas. Letting the mind wander, then, seems to be essential for insight.

To be at our most creative, we need to alternate between periods of tight focus and relaxation.

Innovators talk about focusing intently on a problem and then breaking away in order to have that eureka moment. When you're focusing on a topic, the information that comes to mind first is the stored information that is most closely related to what you're working on. But eventually, you want to come up with something that has been considered unrelated up to this point. When you focus too tightly on what you already know, you may never get to those unrelated, but potentially breakthrough ideas that are remotely stored in the brain.

The renowned physicist Albert Einstein is reported to have said that he would work really hard on a problem, and when he would get stuck, he'd go sailing. The solution would often come to him while he was on the water. According to Jonah Lehrer's article, the mathematician Poincaré reported that one of his biggest advances came to him the moment he boarded a bus after working hard on a problem. Poincaré suggested that you should immerse yourself in a problem until you hit an impasse, and then distract yourself by going for a walk or taking a trip.

■ Different Approaches to Breaking Away

You may remember from college psychology that if you want to study for a test, you do much better if you cut your studying into shorter sessions with breaks in between ("spaced practice") than if you do all of your studying in one sitting ("massed practice"). The brain needs time to absorb and consolidate information, and the breaks allow it to do this. Memory consolidation is more likely to take place if there are breaks in the input of information. This suggests that a workaholic who doesn't look up until a project is done is likely to be less effective than a person who takes regular breaks.

Taking breaks should not be confused with being constantly interrupted, however. Breaks should not come too frequently or just because someone wants to get in touch with you. Breaks should be spaced at reasonable intervals that work for you and that make sense in terms of transition points in what you are working on.

Which kinds of breaks are most likely to promote creativity? First of all, taking a break that brings in a lot of contrasting information is not likely to promote creativity. It may feel good to take your break by checking your emails or surfing the Internet. However, if you're seeking a creative solution, adding more information of a different type will not free up your mind to sort through the information you're working on and find new connections. Breaking away to a lower-information environment is more likely to be productive.

Get a Move On

As the anecdote about Poincaré suggests, simple movement from one place to another may allow your mind to relax and to access remote associations that can be connected to what you are working on. In fact, in *Brain Rules*, brain researcher John Medina reports that physical exercise promotes problem solving, fluid intelligence, and memory. In explaining why this is the case, he talks about the neurochemistry involved:

> "Exercise gets blood to your brain, bringing it glucose for energy and oxygen to soak up the toxic electrons that are left over. It also stimulates the protein that keeps neurons connecting."

Medina suggests putting treadmills in classrooms and offices to encourage exercise breaks. He even proposes that people use treadmills (walking at a very slow rate) during business meetings, while accessing email, and while listening to lectures! The goal is to continually refresh the oxygen that gets to your brain.

Another approach to brain-enhancing breaks is to engage in physical games and activities that are not mentally taxing and that don't involve further information-laden input. Creative companies like Google are well known for providing options like Ping-Pong, yoga balls and rock band equipment for their creative workers to use during breaks. These activities allow for a change of focus while not providing a great deal of cognitive distraction from the problems people are working on.

But even if options like exercise equipment or games are not available to you, walking is almost always an option. If it means simply taking a walk within in the building where you work, that will be much better than sitting still. Moving around during your break will help you take that next creative step.

Nature Nurtures Creativity

When you break away and move around, is there a particular type of environment that is most conducive to creativity and productivity? I talked in Chapter 2 about two types of attention. *Involuntary attention* occurs for evolutionary reasons whenever we encounter something loud or bright or new or fast changing, and these types of elements abound in our environment when we're interacting with technology. In contrast, *directed attention* refers to the more sustained focus we give to projects we are working on. Over time, directed attention is subject to fatigue, and researchers have looked at the types of environments that are most likely to restore our ability to focus.

One area that has been well documented to restore people's attention capabilities is the natural environment. Research shows that turning to nature is a great way to take a break from work. For someone suffering from mental fatigue, exposure to nature restores the brain's cognitive functioning very effectively.

In one study, participants were given a series of difficult tasks in order to produce a state of mental exhaustion. Then, half of them took a walk in a natural area, an arboretum, while the other half walked in a downtown area for the same amount of time. Afterwards, the people who had walked in nature scored significantly higher than the city walkers on a test involving working memory. In a second study, the "natural environment" was simply a ten-minute slide-show of pictures of nature, which was compared to a similar slide-show of pictures of cities, and surprisingly, the pictures of nature produced the same enhancement that walking in nature had. In addition, participants who had watched the nature slides did better than the city watchers on a test that involved executive function—responding quickly to a visual task in the presence of distracting information.

Walking in a park refreshes the brain better than walking on a city street.

Another study showed the beneficial effects of nature using a more practical, real-world task, proofreading. Participants engaged in mentally fatiguing tasks before walking in a park with a stream, shrubs and flowers; walking in a mixed residential and commercial area of a city; or passively relaxing (listening to soft music and reading magazines). Afterwards, those who had walked in nature did a much better job of proofreading than the other two groups.

Theorists contend that nature has a great capacity to restore attention because it attracts involuntary attention *modestly* (with relatively quiet noises and minor changes), in contrast to a city environment that captures attention *dramatically* (with car horns, flashing lights, and the hustle-bustle of city activity). In order to be restorative, goes the argument, an environment must provide interesting stimulation, but at a low level, to allow the brain to recover. It is remarkable that even pictures of nature did this better than pictures of cities.

Communing with nature should also provide the type of relaxation that allows creative people to loosen their tight focus on a problem and identify more remote associations. This is what Einstein must have known intuitively when he went sailing during a project. A more stimulating environment might allow you to shift focus, but it would probably not be as amenable to the discovery of remote connections related to the problem you're working on.

Based on these studies and this reasoning, a great way to take a creativity-promoting break is to find a way to interact with nature. If you can take a walk, try to make it as far as a park if you can, rather than limiting yourself to an area confined to mortar and bricks. If you can't go outside, you will benefit from having a nice view from your office, or at least walking to a window or a vantage point that has one. Perhaps even flowers on your desk or pictures of nature would be better than staring only at office equipment, file folders, staplers, and pencils. It might *feel* better, too.

The notion of breaking away and exposing yourself to mild rather than dramatic stimulation suggests that a ride in a car might also promote productivity and creativity. I myself have found that driving in my car with the radio off allows me to mull over ideas and plans in a way that just sitting in my office or participating in more mentally taxing activities does not. Driving a car forces you to pay attention to what's going on around you and to respond to it, but it still leaves some processing capacity for ideas to ruminate, bump up against one another, and sometimes produce new insights. Even using your daily commute to think over what's in store for your day and then thinking through what has transpired on the way home can be helpful.

Yes, Sleep on It!

There is a burgeoning area of research on the benefits and functions of sleep, not just for health and well-being but for learning and creativity. For years, scientists thought that the function of sleep was merely to rest the body and mind, but recent research suggests that the mind is very active during sleep and that sleep is essential for both learning and creativity.

You will not be surprised to hear that people who are well rested learn better and are more creative and that sleep-deprivation interferes with just about everything. In other words, fatigue is a bad thing. What you may find new, however, is the value of sleeping *after* learning something or during a break in trying to solve a problem. This research applies to both cognitive learning (gaining knowledge of words and relationships) and physical learning (becoming skilled at performing movements or learning new procedures).

Studies have looked at the benefits of taking naps as well as sleeping through the night.

Researchers have discovered that the brain becomes very active when you sleep, and that during certain phases of sleep, your brain becomes even more active if you have just learned something new. In an early study that identified this process, rats were hooked up to wires that measured the electrical activity of their brains while they learned a maze. Later, when the rats were sleeping, the researchers noticed that their brains were emitting the same pattern of activity that they had emitted when they were learning the maze. Apparently, the rats' brains were "re-running" the maze in their sleep and using this time to consolidate their memories of what they had learned. These rats performed well in the maze after waking. Rats that were prevented from re-running the maze during sleep did not perform well.

During certain phases of sleep, your brain works on processing what you have learned recently.

This same phenomenon has been observed in human learning. In one study, participants were given a chance to learn new information. Half of them took a nap between learning and testing and the others did not. Those who took a nap scored better. It has also been shown that the more people's brains replay the activity during sleep, the better they perform on that activity after waking. Apparently, what is happening is not only that the brain practices what it has learned; the connections in the brain are actually being restructured; that is, important connections are being strengthened and irrelevant associations are being weakened.

So if you learn something and then sleep on it, what you've learned will become clearer just as a function of sleeping—compared to passing the same amount of time awake. But even more important for the issue of creativity, sleeping on a problem helps people find better solutions. In a study titled "Sleep Inspires Insight," participants were given puzzles to solve that involved finding the final number to complete a series of eight digits. The way they were trained to solve the puzzle was to compare every two-digit pair in the series. Unbeknownst to them, there was a shortcut to solving the problem that allowed people to identify the solution after only two steps. Participants performed three trials of the puzzle and then were given an eight-hour break before returning for ten more trials. Some of them were allowed to sleep during the break and some were not. The people who slept between the two sessions of the task were twice as likely as the others to discover the easier way to solve the problem. It was critical, though, that the sleep came after a few trials at the puzzle and not before starting it. According to the researchers, sleeping on a problem apparently allows for a restructuring of the brain connections, "setting the stage for the emergence of insight."

Sleeping on a problem helps you find better solutions.

What are the implications of this fascinating research on sleep and learning? Should we recommend that businesses encourage their workers to nap on company time? Brain researcher John Medina recommends that businesses promote midday naps as a way to promote peak performance. Given our current 24/7-multitasking culture, however, I don't expect the business nap to take over corporate America any time soon. However, people working out of their homes might consider trying a nap to see if it works for them.

A solution that would be easier to adopt both inside and outside the workplace is to incorporate a good night's sleep into the schedule of even a small project. Work on anything involving problem solving or creativity will benefit from the ability to sleep on it. I myself find that whenever I'm writing a book, an article, or a keynote, ideas come to me overnight. Often, just as relaxation sets in and I am about to drift off to sleep, a good idea surfaces. Also, I find that a new approach often hits me just as I'm waking up. I've learned to keep a pad and pencil at my bedside to jot down these ideas before they disappear from working memory and get lost.

■ In Short: Don't Be a Workaholic

The great news in all of this new research is that workaholism is highly overrated. Some of the best things you can do to stoke your creativity (and also improve your productivity) are things that are easy and that feel good, and that you might otherwise feel guilty about—taking breaks, moving around, even sleeping! If you're interested in outcomes—doing a project well or creatively—rather than *looking like a hard worker*, following this advice should bring greater success. Tables 3 and 4 summarize these recommendations and provide additional strategies for boosting your creativity.

Some of the best ways to promote productivity and creativity are things you might feel guilty about if you didn't understand your brain.

PRACTICAL STEPS ③

Some Brain-Enhancing Ways to Promote Creativity

- Immerse yourself in as much information as you can for a sustained period, but know when to stop gathering new information and start looking for connections within what you have.
- When you hit an impasse, break away to relax your intense focus on the information you have collected.
- Choose a break of the low-information variety (avoid TV, the Internet, messaging); don't just add more information to an already overwhelmed memory capacity
- Involve some form of physical exercise in your break, be it walking on a treadmill, playing Ping-Pong, taking a walk outside, or even walking around in your office building.
- If possible, take your break in a natural environment like a park or the woods.
- Find a way to introduce a time for sleep within your creative process. This could mean taking a nap, or simply making sure that your project carries over from one day to the next, and that you return to your project first thing in the morning.

PRACTICAL STEPS ❹

Other Suggestions for Enhancing Creativity

- Talk to people about your ideas—especially people outside your area of expertise. Their "naïve" questions on your subject may stimulate you to think in new directions.

- If you can't actually talk to people outside your company, just visualize that conversation, imagining how you would explain your ideas to a specific person and how they might respond.

- Don't schedule a day with nothing but work. Make sure there are fun, restorative breaks available to you when you need them.

- Enjoy cognitive activities that promote thinking outside the box or looking at things from different perspectives. I enjoy crossword puzzles that include oddball definitions—using words in ways that are unexpected.

- Read books and articles about how other creative people came up with their insights.

- ALWAYS have a pencil and paper or digital recorder with you—to jot down those great ideas when they arrive unexpectedly.

4

"That's Entertainment??!!"
Why We're So Stressed Out

> "Anxiety is so high now that normal samples of children from the 1980s outscore psychiatric populations from the 1950s."
>
> Jean Twenge (2000)

CyberOverload happens at home as well as at work, and traditional media like radio and television contribute to the problem along with our more recently developed gadgets. Even though people have eagerly adopted new technological devices over the last decade or so, they have not reduced their television viewing. According to Nielsen statistics from 2008, TV viewing has reached an all-time high, with the average American watching 151 hours per month, or almost five hours a day. Rather than representing a spike in viewing due to the election or the economy, this amount reflects a long-term upward trend in TV consumption. Looking at all forms of media, the Census Bureau estimates an American's average media use outside of work at 8½ hours per day. This includes TV, radio, recorded music, video games, and the Internet, but not cell phones. Although some of this use may overlap because of media multitasking, the data suggest that Americans are media-connected most of the time they're not at work. What are the effects of this dominance of media in our daily lives?

in 2008, for the first time on record, sales of personal computers surpassed business computers.

Whether you're talking about entertainment media or the news and documentaries, it is clear that media content is full of violence and conflict. Violent entertainment has always been popular, and most newscasts have moved toward the "if it bleeds, it leads" philosophy, banking on the notion that viewers eagerly tune in to stories of mayhem, destruction, and hostility. Most political shows and even many financial news programs have adopted sensational reporting and have come to encourage conflict among their commentators.

Another prominent aspect of our media content is that it's scary. Entertainment is replete with frightening fare, from classic horror movies to dramas about homicidal maniacs, serial rapists, and child molesters. And the news these days—from terror alerts to global-warming forecasts, to predictions of pandemics and more—is anything but reassuring.

How does heavy exposure to these contents affect us psychologically? Can we dismiss what we see as "only entertainment" or "somebody else's problem"? Can we remain detached and unaffected by things that reach us only via the screen rather than in person? And are there any long-term consequences of our viewing choices?

If you understand how the brain works, you will appreciate why your viewing habits are important to the way you feel and to your long-term physical and emotional health. Two important advances in neuroscience illustrate this conclusion.

■ Monkey See, Monkey Practice: An Exercise in Hostility

Researchers have long wondered what makes humans so predisposed to imitate each other. Quite by accident in the late 1980s an Italian researcher noticed that monkeys possess what have come to be called *mirror neurons,* cells in the brain that fire when a particular action is performed, but

that also fire when that same action is observed being performed by someone else. Since that early finding, researchers have discovered that humans have a mirror neuron system, too. What's interesting about mirror neurons is that they are located in an area of the brain known as the *premotor cortex.* As its name implies, this is the area of the brain that is involved when we get ready to perform an action. In other words,

When we watch someone express an emotion, parts of our brain that are associated with experiencing that emotion become active.

it could be said that seeing someone else perform a behavior causes our brains to "warm up" for performing that same behavior.

Over the past decade, there has been an explosion of mirror neuron research using brain imaging. Mirror neurons respond automatically, and they respond to the emotional expressions of other people as well as to their overt physical movements. In essence, when we see someone else do something, or see them express an emotion, our brains mirror some of the activity of the brain of the person we're watching. Mirror neurons are also a social phenomenon—they fire if we see someone pick up a teacup, for example, but not if we see the teacup being moved by other means, such as being raised on a moving platform.

Many psychologists consider mirror neurons to be a huge discovery. One well known neurophysiologist argued that mirror neurons would do for psychology what DNA did for biology; they would "provide a unifying framework and help explain a host of mental abilities that have hitherto remained mysterious."

Mirror neurons may well account for some puzzling human competencies, such as the capacity of two-week-old babies, whose behaviors are otherwise a bundle of reflexes, to copy the facial expressions of their caregivers. And there are mirror neurons for sounds as well as for visual images. In essence, when you hear a word, the part of your brain that would prepare you to say that word becomes active. This may help explain the uncanny ability of children to learn language so quickly, (and without peering into their parents' mouths to figure out how the sounds are made). Mirror neurons also seem to underlie the process of empathy, the fact that we readily take on the emotions of other people. And mirror neurons may explain some of the problems that people with autism have in relating to other people. Some research suggests that they have a deficiency in the functioning of their mirror neurons.

Although the research is still in its relative infancy, the activity of mirror neurons suggests that our brains "pre-practice" any activity that we watch—perhaps making us ready to perform that behavior ourselves. So remember: whatever behaviors you are watching, your brain is, at some level, "practicing."

Neurons that fire together *wire* together.

One consequence of this practicing is illustrated by a popular expression in neuroscience: "neurons that fire together, wire together." This means that if a particular neural pathway is repeatedly fired in the brain, that pathway becomes stronger and stronger and more likely to fire in the future. So the effects of practice are not fleeting. We can establish and strengthen enduring neural pathways simply by watching other people.

Keep in mind that mirror neurons fire in response to all the behaviors we watch. If we watch people performing healthy, life-affirming behaviors, our mirror neurons will rehearse those behaviors. But if we spend hours and hours witnessing violence and hostility, it is those mirror neurons that will get the practice and those neural pathways that will be strengthened. In other words, our brains absorb what we watch, and there are physical traces in the brain that result.

The bottom line here is this: if you watch much mainstream television and many popular movies, your hostility mirror neurons will be well exercised.

■ The Amygdala Never Forgets: The Age of Anxiety

There is abundant research that shows that the more we watch TV, the higher our anxiety levels will be and the more likely we will be to experience sleep disturbances. As a media researcher, I became interested in the fact that seeing one particularly scary program or movie can have an effect that endures for a long time. I have surveyed thousands of people, asking them whether they had ever been so frightened by a television program or movie that the fear lasted after the program or movie was over. More than nine out of ten say yes, and when asked to write about their reactions, many describe the program or movie in vivid detail, even though it has been years since they saw it. What's more, they often describe very intense, and surprisingly long-lasting emotional responses.

What is most intriguing is how frequently people describe what appear to be irrational long-term reactions. For example, the following are typical enduring responses to some well known movies:

Jaws: Whenever I swim in the ocean, or even a murky lake, where I cannot see beneath my feet, I feel increasingly panicky and claustrophobic and in a short time, must leave the water."

Poltergeist: "I now hate watching the shadow of the trees outside of my bedroom window. Even now, I certainly don't leave my TV on after the station goes off the air, and I still always make sure that my closet door is closed before I go to sleep."

It's not surprising that a young child would be frightened by the images of bloody violence or monstrous-looking creatures that are featured in scary movies, but what is really puzzling is why so many adults still experience that fear years later. Why would an adult be nervous about sharks in lakes? Or about televisions and trees? These adults should know, in their minds, that they're safe. Why don't these feelings go away?

Many people who were terrified by the movie *Jaws* as children are still anxious in lakes or pools as well as the ocean!

Research on the neurophysiology of fear answers these questions. According to Joseph LeDoux, the foremost researcher on the neurobiology of fear, two distinct areas of the brain are involved in the fear response: the prefrontal cortex, the area involved in conscious reasoning, and the amygdala, an almond-shaped lower-level area that's important for emotions. When you have an intense fright reaction, the amygdala responds fastest and tells your *body* what to do. It creates what is known as the fight-or-flight reaction: your muscles tense, your heart-rate and respiration increase, and various hormones like adrenaline are released into your bloodstream. Your cerebral cortex takes more time to react. It consciously evaluates whatever it was that frightened you. If it was a loud bang, for example, it checks to see whether it was a gunshot (meaning you'd better do something to protect yourself, and fast), or if it was merely a car backfiring or some other harmless thing (meaning, "never mind; you're not in danger").

LeDoux argues that, from an evolutionary perspective, any species that did not have an effective fear response to danger would not survive very long. So according to LeDoux, there are two important aspects of the way your brain works in fear. First, it reacts fast—if something threatens your life, you can't dawdle before acting. And second, if you survive that life-threatening event, your brain wants to make sure that you vividly remember what threatened you, because you may not be so lucky the next time. Therefore, traumatic fear memories need to be really strong and long-lasting.

Part of our brain works hard to make sure we never forget something that traumatized us.

Research shows that although our conscious memories of traumatizing situations are not always correct and are quite malleable over time, implicit fear memories that are stored in the amygdala are highly resistant to change. In fact, LeDoux says they're "indelible." By this reasoning, if you were terrified by *Jaws* as a child, then when something reminds you of the movie, your forebrain should bring up the interpretations you have had in the intervening years. For example, you may think about how silly you were to be so frightened by that obviously mechanical shark. But your amygdala will send out those fight-or-flight signals that get your body agitated again. Even though you may be swimming in a pool and your forebrain may be repeating the fact that there are no sharks in pools, your amygdala is not listening, and you find yourself uptight, breathing heavily, and eager to get out of the water. LeDoux maintains that when your forebrain and your amygdala disagree with one another in a situation like this, the amygdala usually wins. You have to keep working and working on your conscious thoughts to calm yourself down, but your amygdala can be very persistent in stirring up the bodily re-actions that make you feel stressed even though, in your mind, you know you're safe.

Here are some typical examples of people describing their bodies reacting to memories of movies, even though they know they're not in danger:

> "I am actually getting flushed even writing this paper because I am so worked up as I picture the images that I remember in my head [from *ET*]."
> "My spine continues to crawl today at the thought of *The Wizard of Oz*."

The interesting thing about these responses is that al-though we know that what we saw was just a movie and that the virtual threat we suffered through cannot hurt us, our amygdala seems to react as though we had had a real, trau-matic experience. And it doesn't want to let go. Therefore, if our media diet is full of scenes that really scare us, we are likely to be burdened with anxiety reactions that stay with us and repeat themselves over the long-term.

■ Stress, Stress, Stress

I have just described two findings in neurophysiology that suggest that what we expose ourselves to in the media, espe-cially if it's heavy on negative emotions, has important con-sequences for the way we feel. Feelings of hostility and anx-iousness provoked by an over-attachment to media are likely to produce unnecessary stress in our lives. What's more, it's not just the programs we watch in the media that are contributing to this stress. We are living a "life, interrupted." We're constantly being jarred by electronic input in one form or another. It's "answer that call" or "read that email" or check what your stocks are doing or what's happening on the political scene. We may end up feeling like the ball in an old-fashioned pinball machine, careening, often unpredictably, from one beep, ring, flash, or whistle to the next, and encountering one jarring image or antagonistic sound after another. All of our gadgets, if we let them, are introducing and reintroducing us to layer upon layer of unnecessary stress all day long. We're playing constantly with our fight-or-flight mechanism.

Is stress really bad for you? In a word, yes. Remember that your fight-or-flight reaction is there for a reason: it mobilizes your energy and resources to cope with an urgent threat to your physical well-being. When it operates correctly, this reaction arouses you to quick and forceful action, and then in a short time, when the crisis is over, your body can return to its normal, unaroused level. But when a crisis continues—or you feel like you're confronting a continuing crisis—and your body cannot relax, the enduring state of arousal takes its toll on your body. Chronic hostility, anxiety, and repeated interruptions cause stress, and sustained stress is not only unpleasant; it is strongly associated with poor physical health.

Stress isn't all in your mind—it's all over your body.

A 2007 review article in the *Journal of the American Medical Association* evaluated the research to date on psychological stress and disease. It argued that stressful events lead to physical disease by causing negative affective states (like anxiety and hostility), which in turn affect biological processes such as the functioning of your immune system. These biological effects then contribute to problems like cardiovascular disease, depression, and the progression of HIV/AIDS. Stress also interferes with your sleep and leads to increases in bad habits like smoking and overeating. And as you know, these effects lead to further health problems. It is interesting to note that some of the medical researchers who study the effects of stress on disease use gruesome movies to produce stress.

There is also research linking stress to a deterioration in cognitive functioning. In rats, chronic stress leads to a reduced ability to adapt to the changing demands of a learning task and to a diminution of the areas of the brain associated with decision-making and goal-directed behavior. In humans, stress results in memory impairments and lowers a person's abilities to ignore distractions.

Many people understand the connection between what they eat or breathe or touch and how they feel, but they have a hard time thinking that what they see and hear has lasting consequences. But research **What you see is** shows that what you see and hear produces **what you get.** changes in your brain and body that can be long-lasting. You can't simply will away the effects of media any more than you can will away the effects of what you eat, drink, or breathe.

■ Staying Sane in a Crazy Culture

What can you do to reduce this added stress that comes with your constant connection to technology? In Chapter 2, I talked about reducing contact with your messaging devices and the Internet in order to get more done. But detaching from ring-tones, beeps, and alerts can have the beneficial side effect of reducing your emotional strain both when you're working and when you're not. Repeated interruptions can be stressful in themselves, and when you have your cell phone on all the time, it's not just your friends and favored contacts who can interrupt you. So try to schedule relaxing time away from your phone. And, if you can't do that, try turning your phone on vibrate and making ample use of caller ID to limit your interruptions to those people you really want to talk to. Taking breaks from email can also reduce your stress.

And because of the intense load of hostile and anxious emotions conveyed by television, cutting back on your commercial media exposure can help as well. I'm not saying that you should go into a cave and avoid all news and media culture, but I *am* saying that you will benefit by taking a more thoughtful approach to the choices of the media you consume. *You* should be the one to decide what you watch, and when. If you constantly leave the TV on in the background, what will determine your media input will be what sells the most advertising and attracts the most eyeballs. And I don't think I need to tell you that that's not going to be what's best for you psychologically day in and day out.

Become a Selective Media Consumer

TV is not a bad way to relax after a hard day's work, but if you choose to watch a series about autopsies on homicide victims or a talk show where the guests constantly yell at each other, you're not likely to feel much better afterwards. Some research shows that if you're anxious or stressed, watching cognitively involving game shows like *Jeopardy!* can help calm you down. Travelogues and nature shows have also been shown to reduce stress. However, even within these categories, it's important to choose carefully. If the idea is to relax and restore your positive feelings, nature pro- grams that show predators killing their prey or that focus on devastation by global warming are not likely to fill the bill. In fact, the production values of television itself, with its eye toward quick scene changes, controversy, and conflict, are antithetical to relaxation.

Get your news without becoming miserable, livid, or panicky.

And then there's television news. You may have a daily ritual of a particular news show you watch after work. Or you may have cable news on in the background for hours. As you watch, notice how these shows affect you and decide how much news is appropriate. Of course you want to keep up with what's happening in the world, but perhaps you'll get more of what you want and need to know, and more sanely, by picking up a newspaper or getting your news from the Internet. Another advantage of non-TV sources of news is that you get to choose the stories that interest you the most. This saves you time, as well as the boredom or stress that comes from watching stories you'd rather avoid.

I'm not saying that you should avoid misery and controversy altogether. These elements are important for drama and intellectual stimulation. But you should decide which programs involving these features you want to watch and when, instead of having conflict, misery, and controversy as the constant background to your daily life.

If you don't multitask your entertainment, you'll enjoy it more.

One thing I have found immeasurably helpful is having a DVR (digital video recorder) on my television. If you have one, you can set up your favorite shows to record automatically. That way, whenever you're ready to sit down and relax, you've got something you like. In addition, by watching a program you've recorded, you can skip the commercials. Not only does this save you time, (approximately 16 minutes an hour on commercial television), it also eliminates some of the most annoying content television has to offer. And for people who say they multitask in front of the TV because they're so busy, skipping the commercials can save you enough time that you can watch your program and probably *then* do the task that's waiting. And you now know that you can do that task faster and more accurately with the TV off. Not only that, but you'll enjoy the program you're watching more—especially a drama or comedy—if you keep your eyes and ears focused on the TV, so that you can appreciate the emotional expressions of the characters, the details of the setting, and the rhythms of the action. In short, do yourself a favor. Don't multitask your entertainment. Let your entertainment do what it was intended to do: divert, inspire, relax, and restore you.

In addition to choosing television programs carefully, watching less TV overall should help you relax and leave you time for activities that are better at reducing stress. And beyond cutting back on TV, you can give yourself more time and less stress if you cut back on your Internet use. More and more people are going on the web for fun, to explore what they're interested in or to engage in person-to-person applications, like Facebook and Twitter. Whether this experience is stressful will depend in large part on what you choose to do with the Internet. If you're constantly looking for stock prices or political happenings, then, yes, it will be stressful. But even if what you do on the Internet is just fun, if your time online interferes with other things you want or need to do, the result will be stressful. Many people talk about being addicted to the Internet and find it hard to stay away or to cut back. Recent data show that peak U. S. Internet use no longer occurs at work. It is highest at 11 p.m. Eastern time and stays strong past midnight. So web use is undoubtedly interfering with both family time and sleep time.

Replace Unhealthy Habits with Healthy Ones

But cutting down on habitual activities is not easy. Any addiction counselor knows that in order to break a bad habit, it's necessary to substitute a good one. I'm not telling you to stop watching TV or web surfing so that you can spend more time working at home. You probably won't anyway, and as you've heard in the last chapter, being a workaholic does not necessarily make you more productive or creative.

Fortunately, many of the activities that reduce stress are the same ones that promote productivity and creativity.

Productivity, creativity, and stress-reduction go hand-in-hand.

Choose non-electronic leisure-time activities that you enjoy, like getting physical exercise, doing crossword puzzles or brain-teasers, working on crafts or building projects, or playing a musical instrument. Follow your interest and enjoyment.

Another great stress-reducing tactic is to write about what is bothering you. There's a great deal of research that shows that spending a short time during the day writing about your anxieties can have great stress-reducing benefits in terms of both mental and physical health. This happens even if you never pick up what you've written and read it again.

You can also combat stress by engaging in face-to-face interactions with friends. A phone call or an email is a nice way to keep in touch, but there are aspects of interpersonal communication that are lost that way. You can't receive a smile (or a hug) over the phone, and research shows that both smiling and being smiled at produce physiological changes in the brain that are pleasurable. Even smiling at strangers and being smiled back at have positive effects (… remember those mirror neurons). So rather than whipping out your cell-phone while you're standing in the checkout line, banter pleasantly with the person standing behind you. You'll be surprised how much better it feels.

If you're careening from one activity to the next during the day, try to put free time between your activities so you have time to decompress. You can use that time to sort through what you've just experienced and anticipate where you're going next. This will be much less stressful than if you spend that time returning phone calls or emails. Although listening to well-chosen music on the radio or your ipod might calm you down, allowing yourself to spend some time in silence might be even more restorative.

Meditation is another approach to reducing stress. I consider meditation, which is really the process of disconnecting from the outside world and focusing in on ourselves, to be the polar opposite of media immersion. There are many different types of meditation, ranging from those based on a variety of religions to simple practices involving focusing inward and paying attention to your own breathing. Research has demonstrated that a short course in meditation can reduce stress so much that the results can be measured in terms of greater resistance to disease.

If meditation isn't for you, just practice being "in the moment." Divide your day into various activities, and plan it so that you can focus on what you're doing at any given time and not worry about your next obligation and the task after that. If you take an exercise class, focus on your muscles, rather than using this so-called down time to pull together your shopping list.

Finally, don't feel guilty about doing what you need to do for stress reduction. Reducing stress will make you a more productive and creative worker and a better family member and friend.

Tables 5 and 6 summarize these tips for reducing cyber-stress and for stress-reduction in general.

PRACTICAL STEPS ⑤

Tips for Reducing Cyber-Stress

- Find quiet times during the day when phones, email and other connective devices can be turned off.
- Reduce the amount of time you spend watching TV.
- Avoid background TV.
- Reduce your exposure to TV and radio programs that are stress-provoking.
- Choose content that relaxes, entertains, and educates you.
- Get a DVR for your TV so you can record programs you like and skip the commercials.

PRACTICAL STEPS ⑥

Other Stress-Reducing Techniques

- Gets lots of face-to face contact with people who are upbeat and pleasant.
- Smile at the people you encounter during the day.
- Exercise at a level that makes you feel good.
- Choose stress-reducing leisure activities like crossword puzzles, Sudoku, crafts, cooking, building things, etc.
- Find ways to interact with nature.
- Meditate or at least practice being "in the moment."
- Get plenty of sleep and eat healthily.

Even small doses of these activities can work wonders!

5

"Yes, You Can"
Taking Charge of Your Gadgets and Reclaiming Your Life

"The first step towards getting somewhere is to decide that you are not going to stay where you are."

John Pierpont Morgan

As someone who has spent more than thirty years doing research on the negative effects of the media, I can anticipate criticisms of this book that will claim I'm a luddite who will do anything to stand in the way of technological progress. However, I hope you recognize that this is far from the truth. I love many of the inventions that have flourished since the invention of the personal computer. These gadgets and applications make life easier and better in many ways, and I would no sooner give up email, web surfing, and my cell phone, than I'd look fondly back at an era when women were turned away from fancy restaurants because they were wearing pants. (Seriously, they were!) We've only seen the tip of the iceberg of valuable things that computer technology can do for us. I can't imagine telling anyone to spurn all these wonderful devices and applications.

But these new applications present challenges that must be met because they often interfere with some of the most important aspects of our lives. If it were easy to reap the benefits of the digital world without negative side-effects, there wouldn't be a need for this book. When I was well into my research on CyberOverload, I had a conversation with a professional acquaintance who asked, "isn't it true that with every popular invention, there are doomsayers talking about the imminent destruction of society, and that most of the predicted negative effects never materialize?" I thought about this for a while and then disagreed, stating that both negative and positive effects almost always come about with the advent of new technologies, and that then it becomes a challenge to find ways to manage the negative effects rather than giving up on the invention.

Think about the example of the technologies that have made food scarcity a thing of the past. At least in the United States, food is so plentiful that it has become one of the most important factors contributing to the obesity epidemic and other serious health problems. One reason we eat so much and find it so much harder to lose than to gain weight is that our brains evolved in an era when food was scarce. This is why if we go on a low-calorie diet, our brains cause our metabolism to slow down, reducing our ability to shed those excess pounds. And it's also why when we overeat, the excess calories are stored as fat because in the early days of man, it

was important to have a "spare tire" in case food became
scarce again. Although overeating has become an intractable
problem, no one is urging us to go back to an era of food
scarcity. Instead, health advocates are asking people to cut down on "junk food," to make healthy, nourishing, unprocessed selections, and to increase our exercise. Following this advice would be easy if our eating were totally under the control of a rational brain that made decisions only on

Conquering CyberOverload is like staying slim in an age of abundance.

the basis of what's good for us today. The less rational parts
of the brain set up cravings for foods that are high in fat, salt,
and sugar, and therefore, considerable willpower is needed
for most of us not to gain weight.

I think the CyberOverload situation is analogous to the
food situation. Our brains were not designed for the digital
world. Because of our former need to protect ourselves from
predators, we are easily distracted by the constant input that
the digital world brings to us. Now that virtually all applications are portable, we rarely are in situations where we won't
be distracted. Rather than abandoning our gadgets, the solution lies in understanding the brain and developing habits
that maximize their positive and minimize their negative effects. We want to take advantage of the blessings of easy connectivity and access to virtually unlimited knowledge, while
finding time every day to turn off those distractions and the
accompanying stress when they interfere with other goals
that we have as individuals. The more we know about how
the brain works, the more we can understand what we're up
against, and the more effectively we can create an environ-

ment that nurtures our creativity and productivity while keeping our stress low. But it's not easy because our gadgets are so compelling and so convenient.

I've written this book for people who want it all: The benefits of the digital dream without the drawbacks of CyberOverload. It's a challenge, but at least we have one advantage over the people who are struggling to keep their weight down: We can pick and choose when we want to detach, and even if we maintain our serenity for only a few hours a day, we can make great strides. In contrast, we can't just pick a few hours a day to eat properly; we can't stay slim if we eat healthily twenty-one hours a day and splurge during the other three. Most of the advice I give on conquering CyberOverload will help even if followed for a small portion of your day. Moreover, if you start small, I predict that you will like some of the effects so much, that you'll naturally start expanding the time you spend untethered.

Get the benefits of the digital dream without the drawbacks of CyberOverload.

Most of the suggestions I make in this book I've adopted in my own life. To cut down on multitasking and interruptions, I first changed my email from checking for messages every minute to checking every half hour. After doing this for a while and seeing positive results, I decided that when I was writing or trying to solve a problem, it was better to turn off my email program altogether until taking a break made sense. This less frequent task-switching has made me more thoughtful and a better writer.

Another change I made was switching from a workaholic life to a more balanced one. When I took my first job as a professor, I was single and I had moved to a town where I didn't know anyone. I fell into a lifestyle of work, work, and more work. Weekends were no different. As an assistant professor trying to get tenure at a major research university, you know that you can always do more to make your classes better and you never feel that you've published enough. Weekends were miserable because I would devote entire days to work; but somehow I didn't get that much done on those days. All work but no play made me not very productive, not very creative, and not very happy either.

When I got married, this all changed. I concluded that to be a good spouse, I needed to ensure that my husband and I had time together regularly for fun and relaxation. So, especially on weekends, I limited my work to a few hours a day. What I found was that the time limitations forced me to focus more intently on what I was doing. Suddenly, I found myself more productive and more creative than I had ever been before. And as for my experience with CyberOverload, there have been times when I have obsessively followed news or political stories on television and the Internet, and found that it not only cut into my productivity; it left me so stressed out that I was finding it hard to remember things. I actually began to fear that I was having early-onset dementia. But when I cut back my computer and media exposure, my good memory quickly reappeared. I still struggle one day at a time to find the right balance between the quiet and the connected, but each time I stray too far, I am rewarded with the positive results of pulling back. I find it very encouraging to get feedback from my lecture and workshop attendees who tell me about the positive effects they observe when they follow my advice.

In the end, it all comes down to balance. To be productive and creative, you have to alternate between hard-work times of intense focus and break-away times of relaxation. And to be truly happy in your personal life, I believe you have to have both a job (or a volunteer activity) that interests you and gives you a sense of self-worth, and personal relationships and leisure activities that make you feel good and refresh your spirit. Yes, you *can* have it all if you find balance.

In thinking about all the research in this area, I was reminded of two of Aesop's fables: "The Hare and the Tortoise" and "The Grasshopper and the Ant." Although these stories were written to promote hard work and responsibility, it's clear to me that the overconfident hare and the lazy grasshopper did some things we should emulate, at least at times. If you read these fables in the Harvard Classics version, you'll note that the Hare was boastful of his speed, but the cause of his downfall was that he took a nap. And the Grasshopper? He invited the ant to take a break and sit down for a chat. But we now know that sleep reinvigorates the brain and makes us come up with better solutions, and that taking time out to enjoy interpersonal relationships has positive effects on our emotional and physical health. The problem for both of these characters was not that they did bad things, but that they didn't have balance. All they wanted to do was relax. The one overarching message of this book, then, is to try to achieve

Be the Hare AND the Tortoise; Be the Grasshopper AND the Ant. They all have something to teach us.

balance, alternating between work and play, and between intense focus and relaxation.

I've proposed many strategies in this book. I don't expect anyone to adopt all of them. Try them on for size and see what works best for you. Above all, keep your brain in mind.

Keeping Your Brain in Mind

- When you're multitasking or being interrupted while trying to get something done, remember: **Your brain cannot multitask**; it can only switch tasks rapidly, and by doing this, you lose time, accuracy, and quality, and increase stress.

- When you're trying to think outside the box, remember: **information overload interferes with creativity.** Take well-timed breaks to low-information activities, including exercise, pursuing nature, or even a nap or a good night's sleep.

- When you're choosing media, **remember your mirror neurons and your brain's tendency to hold onto traumatic memories.** Select entertainment media that informs and entertains you, and limit your diet of misery and anxiety to things you really want to see.

- Throughout your day, remember that **your brain evolved at a time that vigilance against predators was extremely important** and that continually being interrupted takes its toll on both your stress levels and your ability to concentrate. Find times during the day to disconnect from your digital gadgets and to decompress.

Acknowledgements

I received so much valuable help in creating *Conquer CyberOverload*. First, I'd like to thank the many attendees at my keynotes and workshops whose feedback, interest, and hunger for more inspired me to write this book. Second, I thank Eliz Greene, my mentor at the Wisconsin chapter of the National Speakers Association, and my other many friends there, whose encouragement and great advice have been essential. I thank my designer Andrew Welyczko for his creative editorial suggestions as well as his captivating images. I'd also like to thank my friends and colleagues who read early drafts and gave valuable suggestions: Jim and Carol Lieberman, Barbara Parisi, and Professor Marie-Louise Mares. Further thanks for their input, enthusiasm, and encouragement go to Seth Hall of the Philadelphia Insurance Group, Laurie Benson, of Inacom Information Systems, Joan Gillman and Belle Heberling of the University of Wisconsin Business School, Susan Schmitz of Downtown Madison, Inc., and Julie Fagan of the University of Wisconsin School of Medicine and Public Health.

My enduring thanks go to my husband Bob for his unwavering love and support, and for the way he helps me (and reminds me) to enjoy every day; and to my son Alex, who supplies me with countless quantities of pride and joy.

Glossary

Amygdala
An almond-shaped nucleus in the brain that is involved in the processing of emotions, particularly fear.

Background Tasking
Your brain can "multitask" in this way. It keeps your heart pumping and your lungs breathing and your body upright and performs many other functions that don't rely on your attentional focus at the same time.

Executive Function
Brain processes that orchestrate your attention, telling it where to focus and what to inhibit at a particular time.

Insight
Suddenly seeing new connections between items of information you already knew.

Memory Consolidation
The process by which short-term memories are stored for the longer term.

Mirror Neurons

Neurons that fire both when we act and when we observe someone else perform an action.

Multitasking

Attempting to do two things that involve attention at once. You can't really do this; you can only switch back and forth between the two tasks, which causes extra mental effort and results in time loss, increased errors, and stress.

Single-Tasking

Something that shouldn't need a name, but it's getting rare. Concentrating on one thing and getting it done efficiently and effectively.

Task-Switching

What we all do when we try to multitask.

Working Memory

(Sometimes called short-term memory.) Brain processes that store and manipulate information for short periods of time. Switching back and forth between items in working memory is like "thought juggling." Working memory is less developed in young children, and it declines with aging. That's why young adults are probably better than others at task-switching.

Recommended Reading

Babauta, L. (2009). *The power of less: The fine art of limiting yourself to the essential in business and life.* Hyperion Books.

Crenshaw, D. (2008). *The myth of multitasking: How "doing it all" gets nothing done.* Jossey Bass.

Hurst, M. (2007). *Bit literacy: Productivity in the age of information and e-mail overload.* Good Experience Press.

Iacoboni, M. (2008). *Mirroring people: The new science of how we connect with others. Farrar, Straus and Giroux.*

Johnson, S. (2004). *Mind wide open: Your brain and the neuroscience of everyday life.* Scribner.

Klingberg, T. (2009). *The overflowing brain: Information overload and the limits of working memory.* Oxford University Press.

Lehrer, J. (2008, July 28). **The eureka hunt: Why do good ideas come to us when they do?** *The New Yorker,* 40-45.

Medina, J. (2008). *Brain rules: 12 Principles for surviving and thriving at work, home, and school.* Pear Press.

Pennebaker, J. W. (2004). *Writing to heal. A guided journal for recovering from trauma and emotional upheaval.* New Harbinger Publications.

Helpful Web Sites

How not to Multitask
http://zenhabits.net/2007/02/
how-not-to-multitask-work-simpler-and/

How to reduce information overload
http://thinksimplenow.com/productivity/
how-to-reduce-information-overload/

How to delete email addiction
http://thinksimplenow.com/productivity/
how-to-delete-email-addiction/

Works Cited

CHAPTER 1
How the Digital Revolution Changed Everything

"The digital revolution is far more significant than the invention of writing or even of printing." http://www.brainyquote.com/quotes/quotes/d/douglaseng100293.html

"The management consulting firm BASEX estimates that unnecessary interruptions cost U.S. businesses $650 billion per year." *The Cost of Not Paying Attention: How Interruptions Impact Knowledge Worker Productivity.* http://bsx.stores.yahoo.net/coofnotpaat.html

"In 2008, a writer for *The New York Times* confessed to his ''techno-addiction''"... Bittmann, M. (2008, March 2). I need a virtual break. No, really. *New York Times,* http://www.nytimes.com/2008/03/02/fashion/02sabbath.html?

"A recent video documentary..." *Disconnected.* (2008) http://www.imdb.com/title/tt1432187/

"The contemporary brain is very similar to the brain of homo sapiens who lived 40,000 years ago..." Klingberg, T. (2009). *The overflowing brain: Information overload and the limits of working memory.* (Translated by Neil Betteridge). London: Oxford University Press, p. 10.

CHAPTER 2
"Now Where Was I ...?": Why Multitasking Is Counterproductive

"Multitasking is the art of distracting yourself from two things you'd rather not be doing by doing them simultaneously." This quote has been attributed to a

variety of people and also used unattributed. For example, here are a few web sites that use it without attribution: http://www.toastershark.com/photoblog/Home/Home.html, http://www.metafilter.com/74295/Interestingly-Im-reading-Lifehacker-while-posting-this, http://www.sandiegomagazine.com/media/San-Diego-Magazine/September-2009/Stop-Multitasking/

"Molecular biologist John Medina ... says 'it is literally impossible for our brains to multitask when it comes to paying attention.'" Medina, J. (2008). *Brain rules: 12 Principles for surviving and thriving at work, home, and school.* Pear Press, pp. 84-88.

"...an exercise I adapted from Dave Crenshaw's book, *The Myth of Multitasking.* Crenshaw, D. (2008). *The myth of multitasking: How "doing it all" gets nothing done. Jossey Bass.*

"One estimate says that people at work change their task focus *every three minutes!*" From Gloria Mark, in Pattison, K. (2008). *Worker, interrupted: The cost of task-switching.* http://www.fastcompany.com/articles/2008/07/interview-gloria-mark.html

"Russell Bishop calls multitasking 'half-tasking.'" http://www.huffingtonpost.com/russell-bishop/is-multitasking-good-for_b_177860.html

"...research has been unable to demonstrate any consistent superiority of women over men in multitasking." See Klingberg, p. 71.

"Researchers estimate that working memory reaches its peak at about the age of twenty-five and then begins a slow decline." See Klingberg, p. 58.

"A study out of Stanford tried to demonstrate that frequent multitaskers would perform better than infrequent multitaskers . . ." Ophir, E., Nass, C., & Wagner, A. D. (2009). Cognitive control in media multitaskers. *Proceedings of the National Academy of Sciences.* www.pnas.org/cgi/doi/10.1073/pnas.0903620106

"A study out of UCLA demonstrated that multitasking and single-tasking involve different brain processes . . ." Foerde, K., Knowlton, B., & Poldrack, R. A. (2006). Modulation of competing memory systems by distraction. *Proceedings of the National Academy of Sciences.* www.pnas.org/cgi/doi/10.1073/pnas.0602659103

"In June of 2008, an employee of Intel reported the results of a pilot study." Zeldes, N. (2008) *Quiet time and "no email day" pilot data is in!* http://communities.intel.com/community/openportit/it/blog/2008/06/14/-quiet-time-and-no-email-day-pilot-data-is-in

CHAPTER 3
"I'm Drowning in It": How information Overload Blocks Creativity

"*Creativity is a lot like looking at the world through a kaleidoscope. You look at a set of elements, the same ones everyone else sees, but then reassemble those floating bits and pieces into an enticing new possibility.*" Rosabeth Moss Kanter. http://thinkexist.com/quotation/creativity_is_a_lot_like_looking_at_the_world/149380.html

"Research shows that ... if [people] are given too many choices, they feel less happy about their ultimate decision and are less satisfied with the decision-making process itself." Reutskaja, E., & Hogarth, R. M. (2009). Satisfaction in choice as a function of the number of alternatives: When 'goods satiate.'" *Psychology & Marketing, 26,* 197-203.

"One consumer study showed this dramatically." Study described by Jonah Lehrer in an interview at the Commonwealth Club, February 19, 2009. http://fora.tv/2009/02/19/Jonah_Lehrer_Inside_My_Mind

"A 2008 *New Yorker* article ... reports what neurophysiologists are learning about that 'eureka' moment." Lehrer, J. (2008, July 28). The eureka hunt: Why do good ideas come to us when they do? *The New Yorker,* 40-45.

"In *Brain Rules,* John Medina reports that exercise promotes problem solving..." See Medina, pp. 27-28.

"Creative companies like Google are well-known for providing options like Ping-Pong..." Roush, R. (2008). Google's Open House: Of Ping-Pong, the Gov, and Four Local Projects. http://www.xconomy.com/boston/2008/05/14/googles-open-house-of-ping-pong-the-gov-and-four-local-projects/

"One area that has been well documented to restore people's attention capabilities is the natural environment." Kaplan, S. (1995). The restorative benefits of nature: Toward an integrative framework. *Journal of Environmental Psychology, 15,* 169-182.

"Afterwards, the people who had walked in nature scored significantly higher..." Berman, M. G., Jonides, J., & Kaplan, S. (2008). *Psychological Science, 19,* 1207-1212.

"Another study showed the beneficial effects of nature using a more practical, real-world task, proofreading." Hartig, T., Mang, M., & Evans, G. (1991). Restorative effects of natural environment experiences. *Environment and Behavior, 23,* 3-26.

"There is a burgeoning area of research on the benefits and functions of sleep, not just for health and well-being but for learning and creativity." Walker, M. P., & Stickgold, R. (2006). Sleep, memory, and plasticity. *Annual Review of Psychology, 57,* 139152.

"In an early study that identified this process [that your brain becomes more active if you have just learned something new]." Ji, D., & Wilson, M. A. (2007). Coordinated memory replay in the visual cortex and hippocampus during sleep. *Nature neuroscience, 10,* 100-107.

"Half of them took a nap between learning and testing..." Mednick, S. C., Cai, D. J., Kanady, J., & Drummond, S. P. A. (2008). Comparing the benefits of caffeine, naps, and placebo on verbal, motor and perceptual memory. *Behavioural brain research. 193,* 79-86.

"It has also been shown that the more people's brains replay the activity during sleep, the better they perform on that activity after waking." Peigneux, P., Laureys, S., Fuchs, S., et al. (2004). Are spatial memories strengthened in the human hippocampus during slow wave sleep? *Neuron, 44,* 535-545.

"...sleeping on a problem helps people find better solutions." Wagner, U., Gais, S., Haider, H., Verleger, R., & Born, J. (2004). Sleep improves insight. *Nature, 427,* 352-355.

"Brain researcher John Medina recommends that businesses promote midday naps..." Medina, p. 167.

CHAPTER 4

That's Entertainment??!!: Why We're So Stressed Out

"Anxiety is so high now..." Twenge, J. M. (2000). The age of anxiety? Birth cohort change in anxiety and neuroticism, 1952-1993. *Journal of Personality and Social Psychology, 79,* 1007-1021.

"In 2008, for the first time on record, sales of personal computers surpassed business computers." Vance, A. (2009, September 12). Goodbye, gobbledygook. PC makers abandoning a sales pitch built on complex specs. *The New York Times.* http://www.nytimes.com/2009/09/12/technology/business-computing/12pc.html

"According to Nielsen statistics from 2008 ..." Gandossy, T. (2009, February 24). TV viewing at "'all-time high,' Nielsen says." CNN.com. http://www.cnn.com/2009/SHOWBIZ/TV/02/24/us.video.nielsen/

"...the U. S. Census Bureau estimates current media use ..." Table 1089: Media usage and consumer spending: 2001 to 2011. Statistical Abstract of the United States: 2008, p. 73. http://www.census.gov/compendia/statab/tables/09s1089.pdf

"Quite by accident in the late 1980's an Italian researcher noticed that monkeys possess . . . mirror neurons." Iacoboni, M. (2008). *Mirroring people: The new science of how we connect with others.* New York: Farrar, Straus and Giroux.

"...mirror neurons would do for psychology what DNA did for biology..." Ramachandran, V. S. Mirror neurons and imitation learning as the driving force behind 'the great leap forward' in human evolution. http://edge.org/documents/archive/edge69.html.

"...the capacity of two-week-old babies ... to copy the facial expressions of their caregivers." Meltzoff, A. N., & Moore, M. K. (1977). Imitation of facial and manual gestures by human neonates. *Science, 198,* (4312), 75-78.

"Neurons that fire together wire together." This phrase has been attributed to Stanford neurobiologist Carla Shatz. See http://alumnibulletin.med.harvard.edu/discovery/sparks/shatz.php

"There is abundant research that shows that the more we watch TV, the higher our anxiety levels will be ..." For example, Johnson, J. G., Cohen, P., Kasen, S., First, M. B., & Brook, J. S. (2004). Association between television viewing and sleep problems during adolescence and early adulthood. *Archives of Pediatrics and Adolescent Medicine, 158,* 562-568.

"I have surveyed thousands of people, asking them whether they had ever been so frightened ..." Cantor, J. (2009). Fright reactions to mass media. In J.

Bryant & M. B. Oliver (Eds.), *Media effects: Advances in theory and research.* (3rd Ed.), pp. 287-303.

"Research on the neurophysiology of fear answers these questions." LeDoux, J. (1996). *The emotional brain: The mysterious underpinnings of emotional life.* New York: Simon & Schuster.

"A 2007 review article in the *Journal of the American Medical Association* evaluated the research to date on psychological stress and disease." Cohen, S., Janicki-Deverts, D., & Miller, G. E. (2007). Psychological stress and disease. *Journal of the American Medical Association, 298* (14), 1685-1687.

"… some of the medical researchers who study the effects of stress on disease use gruesome movies to produce stress." Zakowski, S. G., McAllister, C. G., Deal, M., & Baum, A. (1992). Stress, reactivity, and immune function in healthy men. *Health Psychology, 11* (4), 223-232.

"In rats, chronic stress leads to a reduced ability to adapt to the changing demands of a learning task…" Dias-Ferreira, E., et al. (2009). Chronic stress causes frontostriatal reorganization and affects decision-making. *Science, 325* (5940), 621-625.

"In humans, stress results in memory impairments…" Sapolsky, R. (1994). *Why zebras don't get ulcers: A guide to stress, stress-related disease and coping.* New York: Scientific American/Freeman Press.

"…and lowers one's abilities to ignore distractions." Eysenck, M. W., & Byrne, A. (1992). Anxiety and susceptibility to distraction. *Personality and Individual Differences, 13* (7), 793-798.

"… watching cognitively involving game shows…can calm you down." Zillmann, D. (1988). Mood management: Using entertainment to full advantage. In L. Donohew, H. E. Sypher, & E. T. Higgins (Eds.), *Communication, social cognition, and affect* (pp. 147-171). Hillsdale, NJ: Lawrence Erlbaum Associates.

"Recent data show that peak U. S. Internet use now occurs at 11 p.m. Eastern time …" Labovitz, C. (2009). "What Europeans do at night." *Arbor Networks Security Blog.* http://asert.arbornetworks.com/2009/08/what-europeans-do-at-night/

"There's a great deal of research that shows that spending a short time during the day writing about your anxieties can have great stress-reducing benefits …" Pennebaker, J. W. (1997). *Opening up: The healing power of expressing emotions.* Guilford Press.

"You can also combat stress by engaging in face-to-face interactions with friends…" Thompson, C. (2009, September 13). Is happiness catching? *The New York Times Magazine.* http://www.nytimes.com/2009/09/13/magazine/ 13contagion-t.html?ref=magazine.

"Research shows that both smiling and being smiled at produce physiological changes in the brain that are pleasurable…" Ekman, P., & Davidson, R. J. (1993). Voluntary smiling changes regional brain activity. *Psychological Science, 4* (5), 342-345.

"Research has demonstrated that a short course in meditation can reduce stress so much that the results can be measured in terms of greater resistance to disease…" Davidson, R. J. (2003). Alterations in brain and immune function produced by mindfulness mediation. *Psychosomatic Medicine, 64* (4), 564-570.

CHAPTER 5
Yes, You Can: Taking Charge of Our Gadgets and Reclaiming Our Lives

"The first step towards getting somewhere is to decide that you are not going to stay where you are."—John Pierpont Morgan. http://quotationsbook. com/quote/17136/

"One reason we eat so much and find it so much harder to lose than to gain weight is that our brains evolved in the days when food was scarce." Kessler, D. (2009). *The end of overeating: Taking control of the insatiable American appetite.* New York: Rodale.

"The Hare and the Tortoise." Aesop (Sixth century B. C.). *Fables.* The Harvard Classics. 1909-14. http://www.bartleby.com/17/1/68.html.

"The Grasshopper and the Ant." Aesop (Sixth century B. C.). *Fables.* The Harvard Classics. 1909-14. http://www.bartleby.com/17/1/36.html.

Index

About the Author

Joanne Cantor, Ph.D., President of Your Mind on Media, is an award-winning professor, speaker, and researcher and an internationally recognized expert on the psychology of media and communications. After 26 years as a professor at the University of Wisconsin-Madison, she stepped out of the college classroom so that she could spread the conclusions of her research more widely. She knows that television, computers, video games, smartphones, and the rest of our electronic appendages are profoundly affecting us in ways the average person can't see. Her entertaining and eye-opening presentations combine psychology, the latest in brain research, amusing anecdotes, and sound practical advice for being more productive and creative with our time, keeping our own sanity, and raising healthy, happy children.

Over her career, Dr. Cantor has produced almost 100 scholarly publications. She has also previously written a highly acclaimed parenting book, *Mommy, I'm Scared*, and a children's book, *Teddy's TV Troubles*. Her research has received much public attention. She has appeared on *Oprah*, *Good Morning America*, and many other national television programs. She has testified repeatedly before Congress, and the FCC, and is frequently quoted in the national press. She is currently Professor Emerita and Director of the Center for Communication Research at the University of Wisconsin-Madison. She lives with her husband near Madison, Wisconsin.

For more information, visit her website at www.yourmindonmedia.com.

Order Form

Book: **Conquer CyberOverload**

_____ books @ $12.95 each   _____

Sales Tax: _____
(please add 5.5% for titles shipped to Wisconsin addresses)

Shipping: _____
($3.00 for the first book, $1.50 for each additional
copy shipped to the same address)

Total Enclosed: _____

Please call 608-221-0593 or email cantor@yourmindonmedia.com
to inquire about volume discounts.

Shipping Information (please print):

Name_____

Address _____

City _____ State _____ Zip _____

Email _____

Phone number (   ) _____

Please photocopy this form and mail with payment to:

CyberOutlook Press
5205 Tonyawatha Trail
Monona, WI 53716

Or purchase online at www.cyberoutlookpress.com